WORLD ENERGY ISSUES

GAS

The Clean Fossil Fuel?

JIM PIPE

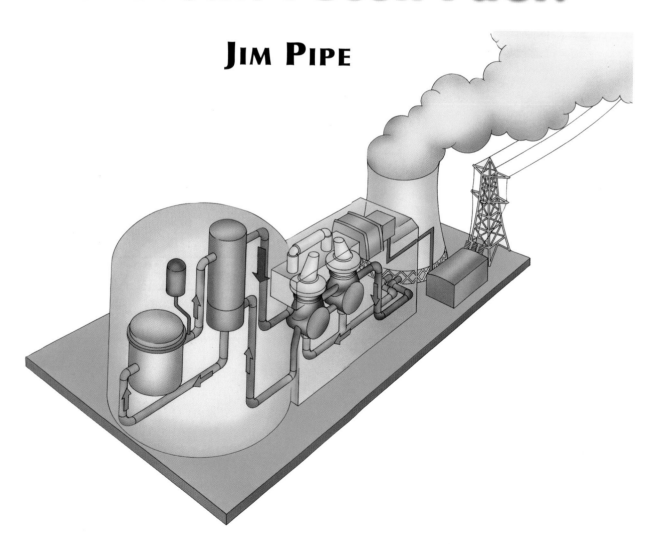

ALADDIN/WATTS
LONDON • SYDNEY

Contents

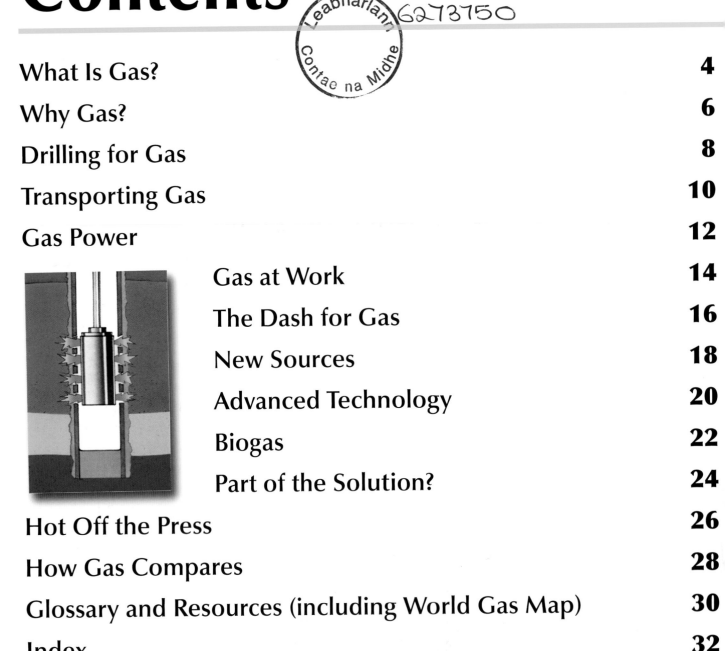

© Aladdin Books Ltd 2010

Designed and produced by
Aladdin Books Ltd
PO Box 53987
London SW15 2SF

First published in 2010
by Franklin Watts
338 Euston Road
London NW1 3BH

Franklin Watts Australia
Level 17/207 Kent Street
Sydney NSW 2000

Franklin Watts is a division of
Hachette Children's Books,
an Hachette UK company.
www.hachette.co.uk

All rights reserved
Printed in Malaysia

Scientific consultant: Rob Bowden

A catalogue record for
this book is available
from the British Library.

Dewey Classification:
333.8'233

ISBN 978 1 4451 0195 8

What's the Issue?

Various forms of gas have been used as heating for over 2,000 years. In the 19th century, a gas made from coal, known as town gas, was used to light streetlamps. Today, natural gas is a major source of energy for heating and cooking. In the future, gas from rotting plant and animal waste, known as biogas, may offer an important renewable alternative.

As oil supplies become increasingly scarce in the next 60 years, gas could help to solve our energy needs while alternative sources such as nuclear, wind, water and solar power are being developed. Though burning gas does contribute to global warming as it releases greenhouse gases, it is much less polluting than burning coal. However, new technology is helping us to produce electricity from gas more efficiently and cleanly.

◊ Dash for Gas

Gas is now being extracted from shale rocks and other unconventional sources on an enormous scale.

◊ Advanced Power Plant

Shuweihat in Abu Dhabi combines a gas-fired power station with a plant that turns 500 million litres of seawater into drinking water each day.

What Is Gas?

Natural gas is a fossil fuel – it comes from the remains of tiny animals and plants that lived millions of years ago. When these died, they sank to the seabed and were covered in mud and sand. Over millions of years, the layers piled up, squashing the layers below.

This pressure slowly turned the remains into oil, which eventually gave off tiny bubbles of natural gas. After forming, natural gas moves up through the holes in porous rocks until it is trapped by solid, hard rock in pockets or reservoirs.

◑ A Blue Flame

Natural gas is invisible: it has no colour, shape or smell. But when it burns it gives off heat and light – a fierce, constant blue flame.

Town Gas and Biogas

Natural gas is made up mainly of a gas called methane. We call it natural gas to distinguish it from an older form of fuel, called town gas, which was made by heating coal. The other main gas used as a fuel is the methane created by tiny bacteria in marshes, bogs and landfills. This is known as biogas.

◓ Gas, Oil and Water

In some places, gas escapes from small gaps in the rocks into the air. When gas is found with oil, it is called associated gas. Natural gas was originally found in large quantities almost by accident when oil companies first began drilling for oil. Gas is lighter than oil, so it rises to the top when trapped underground with oil. Gas is sometimes found with water, too. However, it may also be found without oil or water, due to movements in the Earth's crust that shift the gas away from the original place that it collected.

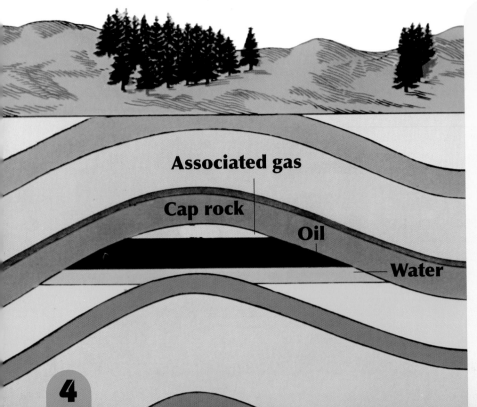

Associated gas

Cap rock

Oil

Water

◓ How Gas is Formed

1 *Dead animals and plants sink down into the seabed.*
2 *The rotting remains are squeezed at high temperatures by layers of rock and sediment above.*
3 *Oil and gas collect in layers deep below the ground. They rise until they reach a hard rock, or cap rock, that traps them.*

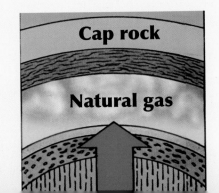

Cap rock

Natural gas

What Is Natural Gas?

Like oil, natural gas is made up of hydrocarbons, chains of carbon and hydrogen formed from the rotting remains of animals and plants. Before it is refined, natural gas is a mix of methane, ethane and propane gases, with methane, the lightest, making up 73-95 per cent of the total.

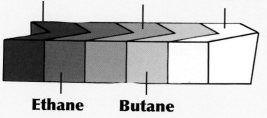

Methane Propane Natural gasoline

Ethane Butane

◐ How Is Natural Gas Found?

The search for natural gas begins with geologists (scientists who study the Earth), who look for rocks likely to contain gas and oil. They study rock samples and measure the Earth's gravity and magnetic field at likely sites. Seismic surveys use echoes from a vibrating pad on the back of a truck to collect information about the rocks below the ground. Sometimes explosives are set off to create an even bigger underground vibration.

◐ Aerial Photos and Test Wells

Geologists scan aerial and satellite photos for tell-tale signs, such as areas where the earth has folded up on itself, forming the dome shape found above many gas reservoirs. If a site seems promising, a test well is drilled.

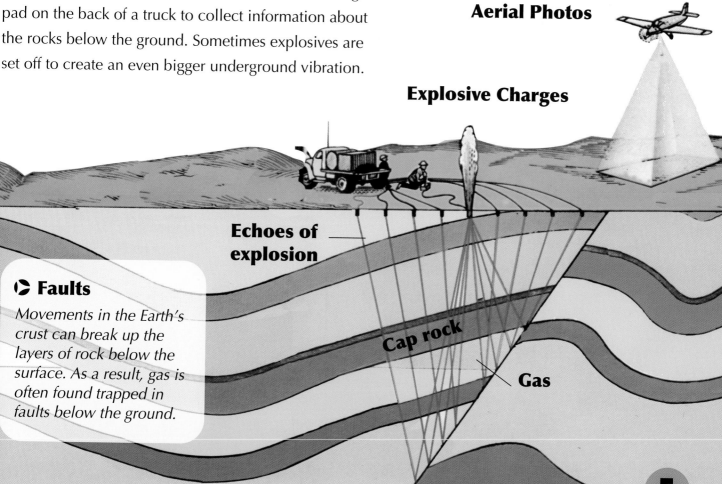

Aerial Photos

Explosive Charges

Echoes of explosion

◖ Faults

Movements in the Earth's crust can break up the layers of rock below the surface. As a result, gas is often found trapped in faults below the ground.

Cap rock

Gas

Why Gas?

Flared Gas. *Often found when drilling for oil, natural gas was once flared (burned off) at the well. This produced huge amounts of carbon dioxide, a gas that adds to global warming. Today, the gas found with oil is captured and used as a fuel.*

The gas that we find underground occurs naturally. It is found on all the world's continents and under the seabed of all the world's oceans. It is an important fuel source and raw material in the manufacture of dyes, plastics and fertilisers.

Natural gas is used as fuel for heating homes and cooking. It is easy to store and can be transported along pipelines. It can also be burnt to create electricity. Gas-fired power plants are efficient and produce relatively little pollution. Meanwhile, new sources of gas are being developed, such as the biogas released by rotting waste in landfills, and the gas created by slowly burning underground coal fields.

Gas storage
This "tank farm" in Japan stores liquified natural gas (LNG) in large tanks.

GAS: For

• Natural gas is relatively cheap. It burns more cleanly than other fossil fuels: it releases 45 per cent less carbon dioxide than coal and 30 per cent less than oil.

• The methane in natural gas is a powerful greenhouse gas so it makes sense to burn it and convert it to less harmful gases.

• New technology means natural gas can now be transported as a liquid in tankers as well as via pipelines.

• Biogas is a renewable source of energy as it is released by rotting plant waste that can be regrown.

• Turning coal into town gas makes it a much cleaner-burning fossil fuel.

GAS: Against

• Even though gas is cleaner than coal and oil, burning gas still gives off greenhouse gases that contribute to global warming.

• Like oil, gas is not a renewable form of energy. When supplies of gas run out in another 100 or so years, that's it.

• Gas pipelines can destroy natural habitats and spoil the natural beauty of a region.

• The gas supply is insecure – gas pipelines are very vulnerable to terrorist attack.

• Half the world's gas reserves are in just two countries, Iran and Russia. This gives them a lot of control over the price of gas.

• Gas leaks, though not common, are potentially very dangerous and can cause a big explosion.

ENERGY FACTS: A Short History of Gas

200 BC Ancient Chinese use natural gas to make salt from salt water. They transport it through bamboo pipes.

200 AD Fire-worshipping temples near Caspian Sea use natural gas in ceremonies.

1600s Town gas first made by heating coal.

1807 First town gas street lights in London.

1821 First commercial natural gas well dug in New York State, USA by William Hart.

1859 First modern biogas digester built in Bombay, India.

1900s Coal gas is stored in towns in large metal gasholders.

1930s Gas becomes a major energy source.

1950s/60s Natural gas fires and boilers replace coal fires in Europe and North America.

2000s Natural gas increasingly transported in liquid form (LNG) in tankers.

2008 New drilling technology allows exploitation of giant shale gas reserves.

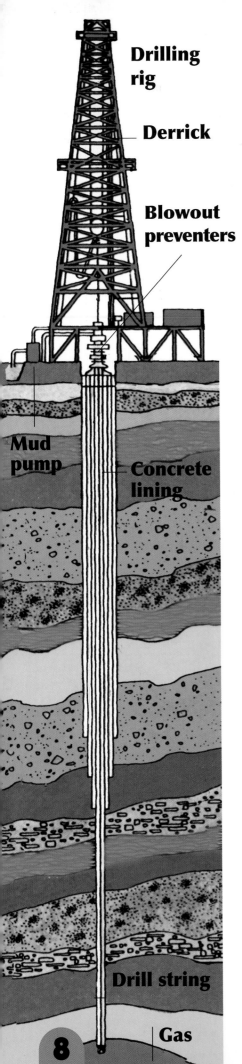

Drilling rig

Derrick

Blowout preventers

Mud pump

Concrete lining

Drill string

Gas

8

Drilling for Gas

It costs a great deal of money to search and drill for natural gas and there is always a risk that no gas will be found. A sharp, rotating drill bit is used to dig down through the Earth's crust. Gas is often found deeper than oil, up to 6 km down, so large drill bits are needed. During a test drilling, rock samples are cut and examined by geologists. If samples suggest the presence of gas, a gun is used to punch holes in the casing of the well, allowing gas to flow upward.

If the flow is strong, a wellhead is built. This system of heavy tubes and valves can cope with the huge pressure from escaping gases and liquids. Now the well is complete and gas production can begin. At sea, giant platforms are towed out to where the drilling rigs have found gas. These can handle the gas from many separate wells.

◑ Drilling Rigs

A derrick up to 70 m tall provides a structure from which the drill string – 9 m lengths of heavy steel pipe – is lowered into the well. If the drill bit breaks, the whole string has to be lifted back to the surface. As the well goes deeper, steel lining is cemented in place to prevent the hole from collapsing. Offshore rigs are used to drill for gas below the seabed. Here there are threats from storms and waves as well as blowouts, when a surge of high-pressure gas blows the drill out of the ground.

▼ **Drill rig** *on Northstar Island off the coast of Alaska, USA.*

North Sea Production Platform

◁ Production Platform

Giant platforms can handle up to 24 wells and weigh over 150,000 tonnes. They are built near land then towed out to sea. Flexible drill strings reach down from the platforms to spread out in the gas field far below, allowing gas to be drained equally from all parts of the field.

▽ Mud Flow

Steel bits are used to cut through most rock, but diamond-tipped bits are used for very hard rock. Fluid known as "mud" is pumped down to lubricate the spinning drill bit, keeping it cool. It also carries pieces of broken rock back to the surface.

Spinning drill

Mud Flow

◇ Perforator Gun

If the signs of gas are good, a special gun is lowered into the well. This shoots through the outer lining of the well, allowing the gas to flow up through piping.

▽ Purifying Gas

The natural gas that comes ashore is a mix of gases and chemicals. It must be processed to remove almost all materials other than methane, the fuel that burns best. By-products include gases such as ethane, propane and butane, and natural gasoline, a liquid that can be used to make diesel (different to LNG, which is natural gas turned into a liquid by freezing).

Transporting Gas

Many of the world's largest gas fields are in remote places such as Siberia and Alaska, so the gas has to travel a long way before reaching the place where it is used. Gas is not easy to transport as it must be pumped along pipelines or turned into a liquid, known as Liquified Natural Gas (LNG), and transported by tankers and trucks. It is often stored underground in mines or caverns for when it is needed, as demand is usually higher in winter for heating homes.

⏷ LNG Tanker

A typical tanker is longer than three football pitches and holds more 125 million litres of LNG. Its insulated tanks work like giant thermos flasks to keep the liquidised gas refrigerated. Safety is a big issue as a single spark could cause a massive explosion. All tanks are fitted with safety valves. These trap any gas that escapes, and use it to power the ship.

Polystyrene-lined tank

LNG

⏷ Liquified Natural Gas (LNG)

LNG is natural gas which has been cooled to its liquid state at -162.2 °C. When natural gas is liquified, it takes up around 600 times less space, making it much easier to store and move around. It can be carried by ocean-going tankers, recognised by their distinctive ball-shaped containers. When the LNG is needed as a gas again, it is simply heated up.

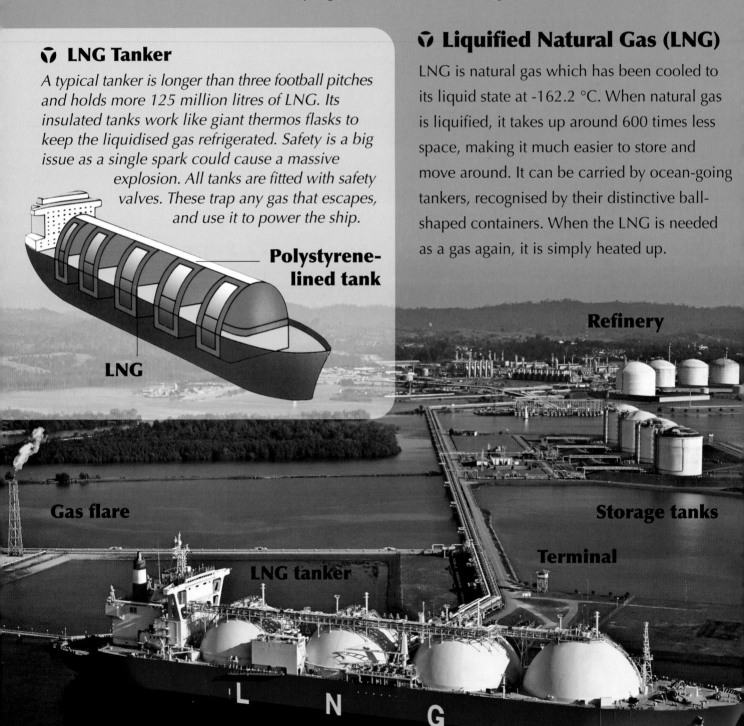

Refinery

Gas flare

Storage tanks

LNG tanker

Terminal

L N G

▶ Pipelines

The Langeled pipeline in Norway runs for 1,166 km and transports gas to the UK. Big pipelines like this can be over a metre thick.

Every 60-160 km, compressor stations push the gas along the pipe at high pressure, creating speeds of around 24 km/h. A special coating stops the pipes rusting while valves allow sections of pipeline to be cut off from the supply to allow for repairs. Intelligent robots known as "pigs" can test pipe thickness, detect minute leaks, and look for other defects inside the pipeline.

▼ Laying Pipeline

Laying pipelines on land requires specialised machines to dig trenches or hold sections of pipe while they are being welded together. A heavy section can weigh 500 kg for every metre of pipe.

▼ Laying Undersea Pipes

To pipe gas ashore from offshore production platforms, sections of pipeline are carefully lowered onto the seabed by ships and joined up by divers or robot welders.

Ship

Pipe

Anchor lines

Gas Power

◭ Power Plant

This combined cycle power plant in Malaysia is powered by two giant gas turbines.

Because it burns cleaner than other fossil fuels such as oil and coal, natural gas has become a popular fuel to generate electricity. The most basic plants consist of a steam generation unit, where natural gas is burned in a boiler to heat water and produce steam. This steam then turns a turbine to generate electricity. Other plants use the hot gas itself to turn a turbine, while combined cycle units are both a gas turbine and a steam unit, all in one.

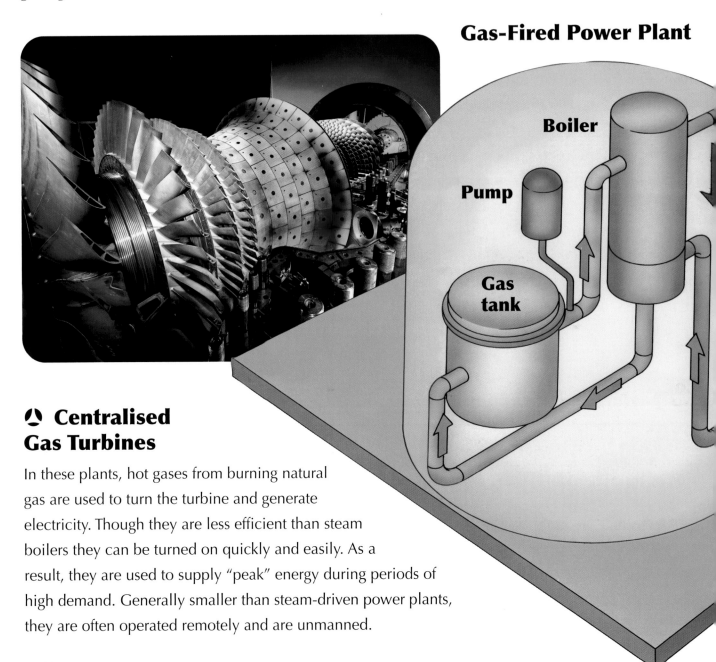

Gas-Fired Power Plant

Boiler

Pump

Gas tank

◭ Centralised Gas Turbines

In these plants, hot gases from burning natural gas are used to turn the turbine and generate electricity. Though they are less efficient than steam boilers they can be turned on quickly and easily. As a result, they are used to supply "peak" energy during periods of high demand. Generally smaller than steam-driven power plants, they are often operated remotely and are unmanned.

✆ How It Works

1 *Gas is burnt and used to boil water to steam.*

2 *The steam is then blasted against turbine blades. As these turn, they drive generators that produce electricity.*

3 *The steam is cooled with water from the cooling tower in the condenser. It turns back into water and is used again in the boiler.*

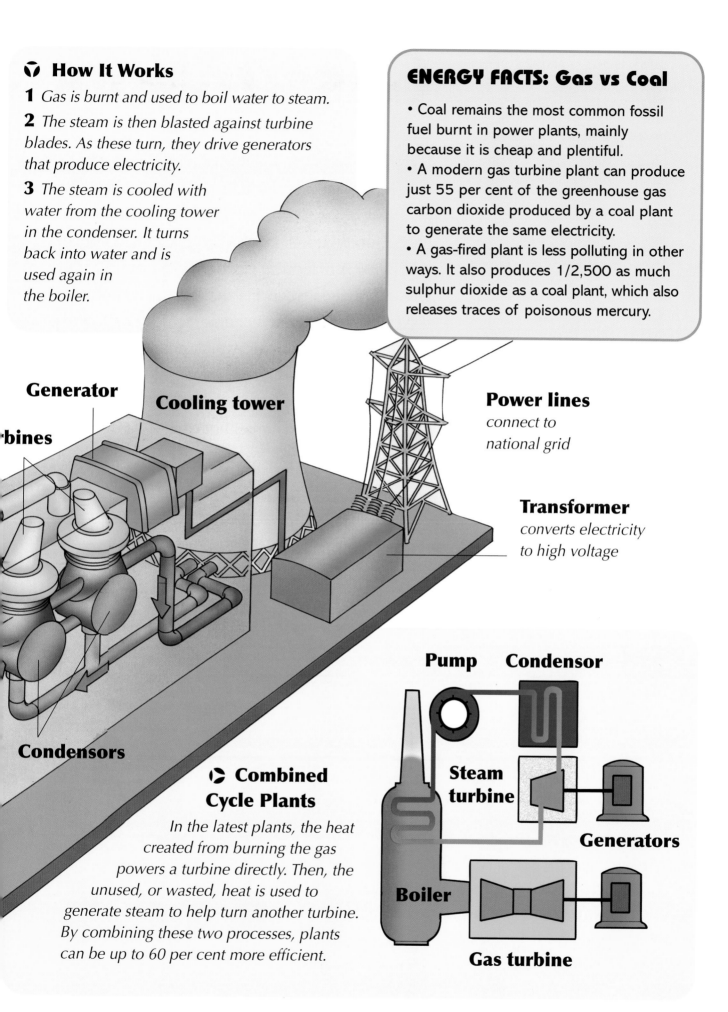

Generator

Cooling tower

·bines

Power lines
connect to national grid

Transformer
converts electricity to high voltage

Condensors

Pump   **Condensor**

Steam turbine

Generators

Boiler

Gas turbine

◗ Combined Cycle Plants

In the latest plants, the heat created from burning the gas powers a turbine directly. Then, the unused, or wasted, heat is used to generate steam to help turn another turbine. By combining these two processes, plants can be up to 60 per cent more efficient.

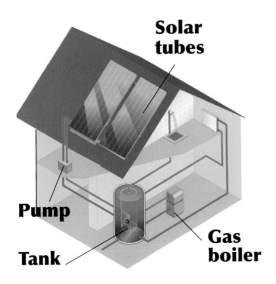

Solar tubes

Pump

Tank

Gas boiler

Gas at Work

Gas-fired furnaces around the world are used in factories to fire pottery, smelt steel and heat glass so it can be blown or moulded. Gas can be piped direct to the factory rather than needing to be stored in piles like coal or tanks like oil.

A network of local pipelines supplies natural gas to homes where it is used for cooking and as a fuel for boilers. It is also used to power air conditioners and fridges in factories and hospitals in remote areas. Two by-products from refining natural gas, propane and butane, are stored in cylinders as liquids and used as a fuel for lighting, cooking and heating for camper vans and homes not connected by pipelines.

◐ Solar and Gas

Some water tanks have two coils so that the heat from solar tubes on the roof does most of the work of heating up the water. This saves energy as the gas-fired boiler is only needed in winter when the water is much colder.

Gas in the Home

In towns and cities, gas runs along a network of underground pipelines known as "the mains". Smaller pipes branch off from the mains and lead to homes and offices. In remote areas where there are no pipelines, houses may have a tank of liquid gas in the garden that is refilled by a gas tanker truck.

◓ Radiators

In many homes, gas is used for central heating. To save energy, modern boilers can be controlled to come on at certain times of day or to heat just part of a house.

Gas Central Heating

1 *Gas is piped into a house from the mains network. A gas meter measures the amount of gas used.*

2 *Ovens burn the gas for cooking.*

3 *A gas-fired boiler creates hot water for two systems, one to heat the house (via radiators) and one to provide hot water for washing.*

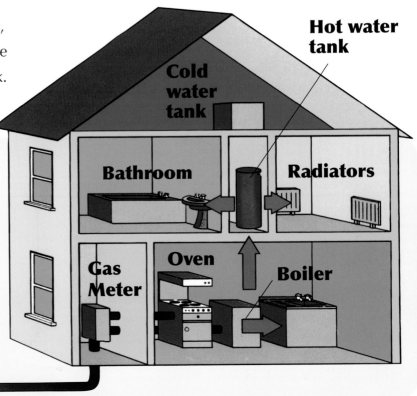

Hot water tank

Cold water tank

Bathroom

Radiators

Gas Meter

Oven

Boiler

Liquid Petroleum Gas

Propane, also known as Liquid Petroleum Gas (LPG), is produced when natural gas is refined. It is a cleaner alternative to vehicle fuels such as petrol and diesel. Some 13 million vehicles around the world run on LPG, which is commonly used in Pakistan, Argentina, Brazil, Iran and India. If oil supplies become scarce, most cars and petrol stations could be easily converted to run on or handle LPG as well as petrol.

▼ Blowing Glass *with a gas flame*

Products from Gas

The gases removed from natural gas before it reaches our homes are used to make a variety of products, such as detergents, glass, steel, plastics, paint and even medicines. The ethane in gas can be made into synthetic rubber. The ammonia created in gas production is used to make synthetic fibres such as nylon. Gas-based pesticides and fertilisers are used on farms.

▶ Synthetic rubber

ENERGY FACTS:
Gas Explosions

Explosions caused by natural gas leaks occur every year. In February 2010, a huge explosion at a new gas-fired power station in Middletown, Connecticut, USA killed five workers and injured 12 others. People felt the blast up to 50 km away. Leaks can also happen in homes. In rare cases it can build up enough to cause a deadly explosion, but generally the risk of using natural gas is very low. Faulty gas heating systems can also cause deaths due to carbon monoxide poisoning, though it is easy to fit detectors that can warn of a leak.

The Dash for Gas

Natural gas could soon become the world's most important fuel, thanks to new technology that is unlocking giant fields of shale gas that were previously too expensive to drill. As a result, countries such as the United States and the UK are planning to replace older oil-fired power stations with power stations that burn natural gas.

Natural gas is also the cleanest fossil fuel, so using it instead of coal will help to reduce the greenhouse gas emissions that cause global warming. Meanwhile, less developed countries are now exploiting the biogas released from rotting animal waste.

Gas Power – Cheap and Flexible

Gas is quickly becoming the number one fuel to make electricity. In the UK, gas-fired plants are being developed to back up the thousands of new offshore wind turbines planned by the government. Gas-fired stations are relatively cheap and can be built quickly. Gas turbines can also be switched on and off easily to cope with peaks in demand and emergencies.

◑ Salt Caverns

With gas use on the rise, salt caverns are increasingly being used as gas stores. Pressurised water is used to dissolve the salt and gas is then forced down under pressure and the water pumped out.

Salt

Gas

Water

World's Biggest Turbine
This powerful German gas turbine can produce the same power as 13 jumbo jet engines, enough to provide a city of 1.5 million people with electricity.

Gas Reserves

Though there are still large reserves of gas worldwide, existing pipelines in some places are close to reaching their capacity, especially those in colder regions where demand is high in winter.

New pipelines are now being built from new fields in Alaska to link up with the network in North America, and also between gas fields in Russia, the Near East and Europe. New terminals for gas tankers will make it easier to transport Liquified Natural Gas (LNG) from Asia and Australia.

Energy Security

Just 15 countries produce over 80 per cent of the world's natural gas, so access to gas supplies has become a cause of conflict in recent years. In particular, in the 2000s, Gazprom, the Russian national energy company, has fought with Ukraine and Belarus over the price of its natural gas. This has led to worries that gas supplies to Europe could be cut off for political reasons.

◖ Russian Rig
A winter drilling rig in Siberia, northern Russia

◖ Global Warming

Like other fossil fuels, gas releases carbon dioxide when it burns. This gas acts like a planet-sized window trapping the Sun's heat and pushing up temperatures. Most scientists agree that this extra, man-made heat is causing global warming. They predict it will cause rising sea levels (due to polar ice caps melting) and extreme weather conditions including floods, more powerful storms and droughts.

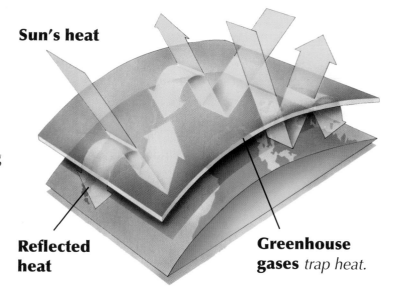

Sun's heat

Reflected heat

Greenhouse gases *trap heat.*

ENERGY FACTS: Rise in Gas-fired Power

- Almost half of the new US power stations planned in 2009 were gas-fired, creating some 12,000 megawatts (MW) of extra power.
- In the UK, the government has given the go-ahead for another 14,000 MW of gas-fired electricity. (1 MW provides enough power for around 600-800 average homes in Europe).

Methane Risk

The methane in natural gas is itself a greenhouse gas far more powerful than carbon dioxide when released into the atmosphere. A tonne of methane in the atmosphere traps in as much radiation as 20 tonnes of carbon dioxide.

Luckily, not much natural gas escapes into the atmosphere – but the more we use, the more risk there is that leaks will happen.

New Sources

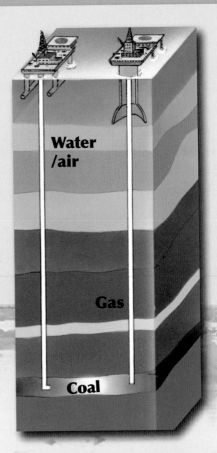

Water /air

Gas

Coal

Thanks to new drilling technology (see page 27), gas is now being extracted from unconventional sources such as shale rocks and undersea coal on a large scale. Meanwhile the gas once burnt off at oil wells is now being turned into LNG so it can be transported by ships, avoiding the need for expensive pipelines. The search also goes on for new reservoirs of natural gas, especially in the Arctic.

⬡ Coal Gasification

Coal reserves that are difficult to reach or mine can be exploited by converting the coal to gas while it is still underground.

1 *Two wells are drilled down to the coal seam, one to pump in a mix of air and water and the other to collect the gas.*

2 *The coal is then set alight. By controlling the amount of air pumped in, the coal only partly burns, so the gas it gives off can be piped to the surface.*

3 *The coal gas is then refined into synthetic gas, like the town gas that lit street lamps 100 years ago.*

This method is now being used in countries such as China, India, South Africa and Australia.

Shale Gas

Shale gas produced from a rock called shale is likely to become a hugely important source of natural gas in countries such as the United States and Canada. To help the gas escape, liquids are pumped into fractures (splits) in the rock and many of the wells are drilled at an angle rather than straight down.

Fire Ice

Huge quantities of natural gas are trapped in a mix of frozen water and methane known as methane hydrates, or "fire ice". This is found under the seabed and underground in Arctic regions such as Siberia, Alaska and northern Canada.

So far, no one has found a cheap way to produce gas from fire ice. Some scientists predict that as the Arctic ice melts, huge amounts of natural gas will be released into the atmosphere, speeding up global warming.

ENERGY FACTS:
Unconventional Gas

Deep gas: Natural gas that exists in deposits 4.5 km or more below surface.

Sour gas: Gas containing large amounts of hydrogen sulphide. The raw gas must be processed, with sulphuric acid created as a by-product.

Tight gas: Gas that is stuck in a very tight formation underground, trapped in dense rock such as sandstone.

Shale gas: Gas found in shale, a type of rock. Until recently, the nature of this rock made it hard to extract natural gas.

⬨ Arctic Ice

There may be enough gas under the Arctic seabed to supply the world for 15-20 years. However, drilling for gas here could damage one of the world's last great wilderness areas.

⬨ Flared Gas Now Used

In the past, the natural gas recovered from oil wells was simply burned at the oil field (known as flaring). This wasteful practice is now illegal in many countries.

Advanced Technology

Scientists are constantly looking for ways to make gas-fired plants more efficient. While Combined Heat and Power (CHP) plants make use of heat that is wasted in conventional boilers, Magneto Hydro Dynamic (MHD) generators turn the heat from burning gas directly into electricity, without needing any moving parts. Other advances include improved drilling methods and converting natural gas into a liquid fuel that can be used by cars, trucks and planes.

Micro CHPs *can be used in homes.*

Undersea Robots

Gas companies are depending more and more on hi-tech robots as the search for gas takes them into dangerous Arctic and deep-sea waters. Undersea robots are used for many different tasks, from inspecting equipment on the seabed to digging trenches for undersea pipelines.

The UT-1 Ultra Trencher is the world's biggest subsea robot. It weighs 60 tonnes and is the same size as a small house. Moving at a speed of over 5 km/h under the sea, it can dig a trench for pipelines in waters up to 1,500 m deep.

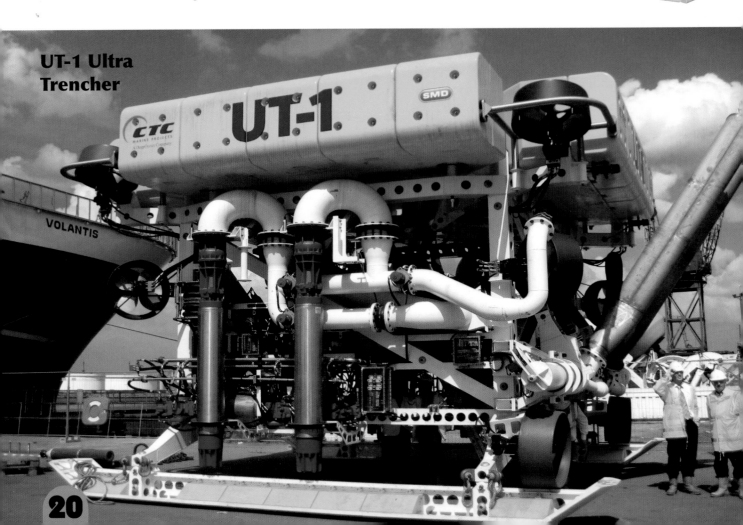

UT-1 Ultra Trencher

CHP plant

⚊ Combined Heat and Power

Like normal gas-fired power plants, CHP systems use a gas turbine to drive a generator, creating electricity. However, they also recover the heat used in the boiler and this can provide hot water to heat a local factory or housing estate.

CHPs are up to 70 per cent efficient, compared with 48 per cent for a gas-fired power plant and 35 per cent for a coal-fired plant. The 160 MW CHP generator at the Baytown Olefins Plant in Texas (above) is large enough to supply the energy needs of at least 100,000 US homes.

▽ Undersea Drilling Rigs

Big waves, frozen machinery and icebergs will be major problems for future offshore gas drilling rigs in Arctic waters. Some firms are looking at remotely-controlled robot drilling rigs that sit on the seabed.

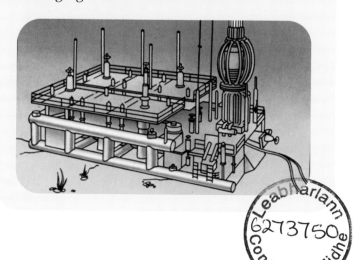

MHD Generators

The MHD (Magneto Hydro Dynamic) generator turns heat directly into electricity. Some fuels burn hot enough to produce a plasma, a gas that conducts electricity. In an MHD, the plasma is produced at high pressure by burning natural gas. This is then directed through a magnetic field, creating electricity like a turbogenerator.

MHDs can operate at high temperatures without moving parts, so less fuel is used to make the same amount of electricity, especially when burning coal or natural gas. This technology has also been used for super-quiet submarine engines.

GTL plant *at Bintulu, Malaysia*

⚊ Gas to Liquids (GTL)

Natural gas is four times more expensive to transport than oil, a big problem given that most big gas fields are in remote regions like Siberia.

One way around this is Gas to Liquids technology (GTL). This converts natural gas into synthetic petrol, diesel or jet fuel using a process first developed in Germany during World War II. These fuels can then be easily transported using oil pipelines and tankers. Giant GTL plants are already in countries such as Qatar, Iran and Nigeria. GTL is also used to convert the gas found in oil wells into liquid, avoiding the need for expensive pipelines.

Biogas

⚠ Seaweed Biogas

Ocean plants such as giant kelp can be turned into methane gas that can be burnt for energy. In the future, huge kelp farms could produce renewable gas energy.

Many countries have no supply of natural gas or cannot afford to buy it from abroad. They make their own gas from animal and human waste. Methane forms when plants rot in places where there is no air. Landfill gas is methane that builds up underground as rubbish is broken down by bacteria. This biogas can be collected. After it is mixed with carbon dioxide, it can be burned like natural gas for cooking or heating, or used to generate electricity.

Biogas can also be produced from animal or human waste in a digester. However, because of its low methane content, this biogas can't be used to fuel vehicles unless it is treated and compressed like Liquified Natural Gas (LNG).

Building a Digester

⟨⟩ Landfill Sites

We can collect gas from landfill sites. Biomass waste, such as kitchen scraps, usually ends up at the local tip. Over several decades, bacteria steadily decompose this organic matter, giving off the gas methane.

This can be extracted by "capping" a landfill site with a layer of clay. Pipes collect the gas and bring it to the surface, where it is processed and piped to homes, or used to generate electricity.

Biogas from Animal Waste

3 *The bacteria produce methane, which is tapped and collected, then piped to homes.*

2 *Bacteria is added to the fermentation chamber.*

1 *Animal dung or human sewage is fed into tanks called digesters.*

⟨⟩ Digesters

Digestion is a way of using bacteria to create biogas. These tiny organisms usually live at the bottom of swamps where there is no air. When they consume dead organic matter, they produce methane and hydrogen.

We can put these bacteria to work by adding them to tanks of human or animal waste, called digesters. Up to two-thirds of the energy of the animal dung is turned into fuel and the remains are used as fertiliser.

ENERGY FACTS:
Energy Poverty

Around 1.5 billion people in the world still rely on wood, animal dung and other biomass for cooking, heating and lighting. Using biogas for fuel is much cleaner and healthier than these often smoky fuels.

Using biogas to generate electricity can further transform life for poor communities. Electricity powers water pumps, radios, telephones and lights for schools and hospitals.

Part of the Solution?

ENERGY FACTS:
A Flexible Fuel

• Gas turbines can be made in many different sizes from giant power plants to microturbines that provide power for six to seven homes or small businesses.
• Local energy grids relying mainly on wind or solar could switch on small gas turbines when demand is high. Small gas turbines could even be used in cars.

Some energy experts believe that moving from coal and oil to cleaner-burning natural gas or coal gas could help in the short term to delay the effects of global warming.

Meanwhile the world is developing clean and renewable sources of energy, such as wind, solar and water power, using gas-fired power plants for extra power when demand peaks. New Liquified Natural Gas (LNG) technology is certainly helping to bring down the cost of gas from remote wells.

It will probably take a mix of gas-fired power plants, nuclear power and renewables to provide for the world's future energy needs. But the answer isn't just about creating more energy – we also need to get the most out of the energy we use.

◐ Local Power Plant

This housing complex in the Bronx district of New York has its own 40 MW gas-fired power plant. Since 2007, the plant has been producing about twice the power needed by 60,000 residents. The extra power is sold off, which should pay for the plant within five years.

Saving Energy

It's much cheaper to save gas, oil and electricity than to extract more fuel from the ground. Today's cars already travel twice as far on the same litre of petrol as cars did in the 1970s.

Modern A-rated appliances use half the energy of older machines. However, houses and cars in most developed countries are generally much bigger than they used to be, wiping out the savings in energy from more efficient machines.

A Cleaner Fossil Fuel?

Gas produces 50 per cent less of the greenhouse gas carbon dioxide than coal and 33 per cent less than oil, so using it will help to reduce emissions. This will not solve the problem of global warming, but could buy us time to create better technologies for renewables such as wind, solar and wave power, which currently supply less than 10 per cent of the world's energy.

▼ More Efficient Homes

In many countries there are now laws and grants encouraging home owners to save energy and generate their own electricity.

• Some methods are simple, such as using energy-saving lightbulbs, insulating roofs and walls or putting in windows that trap heat from the Sun.

• Recycling reuses raw materials and uses less energy than making new objects.

• Creating power locally using wind and water turbines or solar panels will reduce the need for large power plants. It also saves energy as a lot of power is lost when it is carried long distances on power lines. Micro CHP boilers (page 21) can also be used to generate electricity.

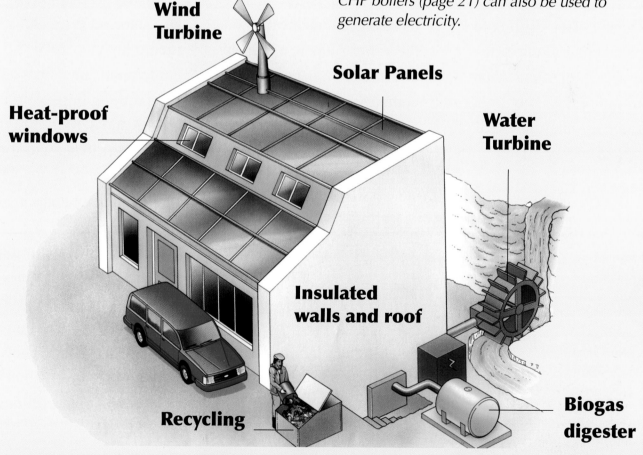

Wind Turbine

Solar Panels

Heat-proof windows

Water Turbine

Insulated walls and roof

Recycling

Biogas digester

HOT OFF THE PRESS

Laser Drills

■ Scientists are now developing powerful lasers that can be used to drill for gas and oil. Fibre optic cables transfer the intense light from lasers on the surface to a series of lenses that then direct the laser beams onto the rock face.

Lasers don't wear out as they never rub against the rock like a mechanical bit. As a result, they cut through the rock quicker as there is no need to stop drilling to replace them. Equipping the laser with sensors that can find rocks likely to contain gas may also save time and energy.

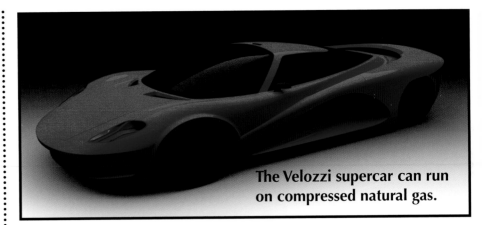

The Velozzi supercar can run on compressed natural gas.

Microturbines

■ Microturbines are miniature versions of the gas turbines used in factories – some are small enough to fit in your hand. In the future, these could power cars like the Velozzi supercar, which can run on propane and compressed natural gas as well as diesel or biodiesel. This car can drive for 320 km on a single charge of its battery – then the micro-turbine kicks in and charges up the battery again.

Drilling Deeper

■ Since oil prices hit record highs in 2008, exploration companies have been drilling further out into the sea and deeper under the ocean floor to tap into some of the last remaining pockets of oil and natural gas in the world.

Ultra Deep Water drilling rigs are simply enormous – they are as big as the Eiffel Tower and weigh as much as 10,000 family cars. They can operate wells over 4,000 m below the surface, drilling into the mud and rock below the seabed.

The Perdido Spar – an Ultra Deep Water drilling rig – being built

Breakthrough in Shale Gas Drilling Methods

■ New drilling methods could open up a vast new supply of gas scattered around the world. This gas is found in shale, a rock that is lightly soaked with gas. As it formed, the gas created tiny splits in the rock. US drilling companies are now forcing water into the cracks at high pressure. This widens the holes and holds them open to let the gas out. Wide areas can be drilled at the same time using "horizontal drilling" – turning the bit at up to 90 degrees when it has reached the right layer of rock.

Drilling for shale gas is messy, however. Millions of litres of water mixed with sand, acid and toxic chemicals are blasted at rocks, and some of this can find its way into supplies of drinking water. In 2009, over 30,000 litres of chemicals polluted a stream in Pennsylvania, USA.

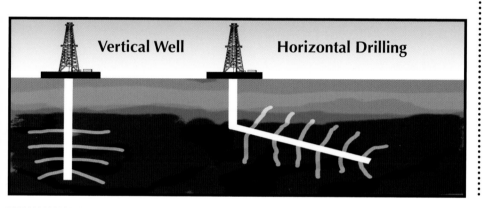

Vertical Well   Horizontal Drilling

Out of a Tight Spot

■ Tight gas are reserves of gas trapped in rocks once considered too difficult or too expensive to drill for – until now. Today, 3-D imaging methods are helping exploration companies to exploit these unconventional gas fields. Known as 3-D Seismic imaging, they work like the ultrasound scans used to create pictures of unborn babies – except they can reach down to depths of over 6,000 m! They give a much clearer picture than 2-D scans, cutting down on the number of "dry wells", where no gas is found.

World's First Passenger GTL Flight

■ In November 2009, a passenger jet flying from London to Qatar became the first to be powered using a fuel made from natural gas.

Until recently, jet fuel was made only from oil. But Gas to Liquids (GTL) technology can now convert natural gas into a liquid fuel for aircraft.

By 2012, a new GTL plant in Qatar will produce around 1 million tonnes of jet fuel each year.

Could GTL become the jet fuel of the future?

How Gas Compares

While gas is the cleanest fossil fuel, burning it still releases carbon dioxide into the atmosphere, adding to pollution and global warming. Nuclear power is one alternative, but reactors are expensive and they create dangerous waste. Biofuels and other renewables are much cleaner sources of energy, but they supply just a small part of the world's energy needs.

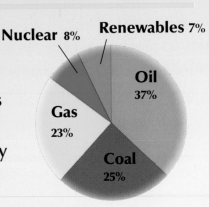

World Energy Sources

Nuclear 8%
Renewables 7%
Oil 37%
Gas 23%
Coal 25%

NON-RENEWABLE ENERGY

Gas

For:
Gas is relatively cheap, and produces less greenhouses gases than oil and coal.

Against:
Burning gas releases carbon dioxide. Gas is not renewable and the world's natural gas reserves are limited. Gas pipelines can disrupt the migration routes of animals such as caribou.

Oil

For:
Oil is cheap and easy to store, transport and use.

Against:
Oil is not renewable and it is getting more expensive to get out of the ground. Burning oil releases large amounts of greenhouse gases. Oil spills, especially at sea, cause severe pollution.

Coal

For:
Coal is cheap and supplies of coal are expected to last another 150 years.

Against:
Coal-fired power stations give off the most greenhouse gases. They also produce sulphur dioxide, creating acid rain. Coal mining can be very destructive to the landscape.

Nuclear

For:
Nuclear power is constant and reliable, and doesn't contribute to global warming.

Against:
Not renewable as uranium (the main nuclear fuel) will eventually run out. Nuclear waste is so dangerous it must be buried for thousands of years. Also the risk of a nuclear accident.

Solar Power

For:

Solar power needs no fuel, it's renewable and doesn't pollute.

Against:

Solar power stations are very expensive as solar (photovoltaic) cells cost a lot compared to the amount of electricity they produce. They're unreliable unless used in a very sunny climate.

Wind Power

For:

Wind power needs no fuel, it's renewable and doesn't pollute.

Against:

Wind is unpredictable, so wind farms need a back-up power supply. Possible danger to bird flocks. It takes thousands of wind turbines to produce the same power as a nuclear plant.

Hydroelectric Power

For:

Hydroelectric power needs no fuel, is renewable and doesn't pollute.

Against:

Hydro-electric is very expensive to build. A large dam will flood a very large area upstream, impacting on animals and people there. A dam can affect water quality downstream.

Geothermal Power

For:

Geothermal power needs no fuel, it's renewable and doesn't pollute.

Against:

There aren't many suitable places for a geothermal power station as you need hot rocks of the right type and not too deep. It can "run out of steam". Underground poisonous gases can be a danger.

Biofuels

For:

Biofuels are cheap and renewable and can be made from waste.

Against:

Growing biofuels from energy crops reduces the land available for food and uses up vital resources such as fresh water. Like fossil fuels, biofuels can produce greenhouse gases.

Tidal Power

For:

Tidal power needs no fuel, is reliable, renewable and doesn't pollute.

Against:

Tidal power machines are expensive to build and only provide power for around 10 hours each day, when the tide is actually moving in or out. Not an efficient way of producing electricity.

Glossary and Resources

atmosphere The thick blanket of air that surrounds the Earth.

biogas Gas, especially methane, produced from plant and animal matter.

bit The sharp tool on the end of a drill that cuts through the rock.

CHP Combined Heat and Power, a power station that produces both electricity and heat for a local district.

climate The average weather in a region over a long period of time.

condense To change from gas to liquid.

decompose To rot.

derrick The steel frame that holds the drilling equipment at a well.

digester A tank in which biomass rots and gives off biogas.

drill string A set of linked steel pipes that are attached to a drill bit.

extract To take something out.

fossil fuel A fuel such as coal, oil or gas that is formed underground from the remains of prehistoric plants and animals.

gas field A region with large reserves of gas ready to be extracted.

gas rig A platform used to drill for gas offshore.

gas to liquids technology (GLT) A process that converts natural gas into petrol, diesel or jet fuel.

generator A machine that turns mechanical energy into electrical energy.

geologist A scientist who studies the Earth.

global warming A warming of the Earth's surface. Many scientists predict that global warming may lead to more floods, droughts and rising sea levels.

greenhouse effect The global warming caused by human-made gases, such as carbon dioxide and methane, that trap the heat from the Sun in the atmosphere.

liquid petroleum gas (LPG) A by-product of gas production, this liquid fuel can be used in cars and trucks.

liquified natural gas (LNG) Natural gas that has been turned into a liquid.

megawatt (MW) A million watts (a watt is a unit of power). A gigawatt is 1,000 MW.

offshore At sea, not far from the coast.

power station A plant where electricity is generated.

production platform A platform that pumps gas from below the seabed.

renewable Something that can be used over and over without running out.

turbine A machine with rotating blades.

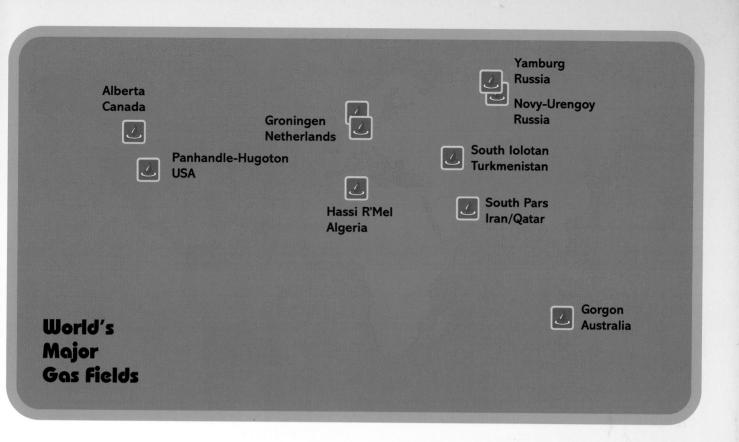

Alberta
Canada

Panhandle-Hugoton
USA

Groningen
Netherlands

Hassi R'Mel
Algeria

Yamburg
Russia

Novy-Urengoy
Russia

South Iolotan
Turkmenistan

South Pars
Iran/Qatar

Gorgon
Australia

World's
Major
Gas Fields

Useful Websites

If you're interested in finding out more about natural gas and biogas, the following websites are helpful:

www.naturalgas.org
www./tonto.eia.doe.gov/kids/energy
www.domsafety.com/schools/engsw/
   landing2.html
www.carbonkids.net/kids_fossilfuels.html
www.therenewableenergycentre.co.uk
www.alternative-energy-news.info/
   technology/biofuels/

ENERGY FACTS:
Top Ten Gas Producing Nations

The ten countries producing the most gas in 2008 were:

1 **Russia** – 662 billion cubic metres
2 **United States** – 582 billion cubic metres
3 **Canada** – 170 billion cubic metres
4 **Iran** – 116 billion cubic metres
5 **Norway** – 99 billion cubic metres
6 **Algeria** – 87 billion cubic metres
7 **Netherlands** – 85 billion cubic metres
8 **Saudi Arabia** – 80 billion cubic metres
9 **Qatar** – 77 billion cubic metres
10 **China** – 76 billion cubic metres

Further reading

World Issues: Energy Crisis by Ewan McLeish (Aladdin/Watts)
Our World: Gas by Sarah Levete (Aladdin/Franklin Watts)
Earth's Resources: Oil Gas by Neil Morris (Franklin Watts)
Energy Files: Oil and Gas by Steve Parker (Heinemann Library)
Sources of Energy: Fossil Fuels by Diane Gibson (Creative Company)
Issues in Our World: Energy Crisis by Ewan McLeish (Aladdin/Watts)

Index

Photocredits

(Abbreviations: t – top, m – middle, b – bottom, l – left, r – right).

All photos istockphoto.com except: 3b: Nordex GmbH. 10b, 16-17: Siemens press picture. 13br: courtesy AMEC. 15tr & 15br: courtesy Quiet Revolution. 18tl and 19tr: Proven Energy. 19tl: The International Polar Foundation. 20b: Michael Svoboda/dreamstime.com. 22tl: BARD Engineering GmbH/Lang. 23t: courtesy StatoilHydro. 23br: courtesy General Compression. 25tl: courtesy Magenn Power Inc. 25bl: courtesy SkySails GmbH. 26br: courtesy Fraunhofer Institute. 26t: Windation Energy Systems, Inc. 27tr: Green Ocean Energy Ltd. 27b: courtesty www.metropolismag.com.